BEYLERBEYİ PALACE

TBMM DEPARTMENT OF NATIONAL PALACES

BEYLERBEYİ PALACE

A PUBLICATION OF THE TBMM DEPARTMENT OF NATIONAL PALACES

İSTANBUL 1993

PUBLICATION NO. 6 OF THE TBMM DEPARTMENT OF NATIONAL PALACES

EDITED AND DESIGNED BY THE DEPARTMENT OF PALACES
AND KÖŞKS, 1992 PUBLISHED WITH THE FINANCIAL SUPPORT
OF THE TBMM FOUNDATION

PUBLISHING COORDINATOR İHSAN YÜCEL
DESIGN ERSU PEKİN
TEXT HAKAN GÜLSÜN
TRANSLATION PRISCILLA MARY IŞIN
EDITORIAL TEAM AYDAN GÜRÜN, ESİN ÖNCÜ, FERDA ULUGERGERLİ
PHOTOGRAPHY SAMİH RIFAT, FİKRET YILDIZ
TYPESETTING NATIONAL PALACES DATA PROCESSING CENTRE
COLOUR SEPARATION OFSET YAPIMEVİ
PRINTED BY TBMM BASIMEVİ

ISBN 975-95334-7-2

Contents

FOREWORD

T he palaces which were not only the residences of the Ottoman sultans but centres of government for the Ottoman Empire, and the smaller köşks and kasırs which the sultans used for recreation became the property of the nation on 3 March 1924, shortly after the establishment of the Turkish Republic.

Today administered by the Department of National Palaces, which is directly attached to the Turkish Grand National Assembly, these imperial buildings are known collectively as the National Palaces and open to the public as museum-palaces. They are each a highly significant focal point of history, throwing light on the social structure, government, art and culture of Ottoman society.

Obtaining detailed and reliable knowledge of these buildings, which were not only residences of the Ottoman sultans but centres of government until the early years of this century, depends on extensive research. This publication, while inevitably limited in scope, is nevertheless a valuable source of information about Beylerbeyi Palace and its role in Ottoman administrative structure, social life, culture and art. Reference to this information in future publications will undoubtedly help to bring to light further details about İstanbul's other imperial buildings.

I hope that readers will enjoy this book, and that further planned National Palaces publications will play a role in the understanding and conservation of our national heritage. I also take this opportunity to thank all those who have contributed to its publication.

TÜRKÂN İNCE
Director
Department of National Palaces

BEYLERBEYI PALACE
FROM PAST TO PRESENT

*T*he area between Kuzguncuk and Çengelköy on the Asian shore of the Bosphorus has been settled since Byzantine times, although whether as a summer resort or as a sanctuary is unclear. However, it is quite likely that by establishing an imperial estate or hasbahçe here the Ottoman sultans were carrying on a tradition dating from the Byzantines.

The pre-Ottoman name of the area is as disputed as its function. The 17th and 18th century writers, Kömürcüyan and İnciciyan, record that it was named İstavroz, and mention the existence of a domed church. According to İnciciyan, the name İstavroz derives from a cross erected here by Constantine the Great. Another 17th century writer, Evliya Çelebi, tells us that the name comes from İstavrit (horse mackerel), which was plentiful in the sea here. The origin of the present name Beylerbeyi is equally a matter for conjecture. As late as 1802, the records of the Bostancıbaşı (commander of the Imperial guard who had jurisdiction over the shores and waters of the Bosphorus) give the name as İstavroz, although İnciciyan tells us that the name Beylerbeyi dates back to the 16th century, when Beylerbeyi (governor-general)

Detail from a sketch by J. Schranz of Old Beylerbeyi Palace, whose "profusion of windows" is noted by Moltke in his memoirs (late 18th C.).

Mehmed Paşa had a house here. The *"Boğaziçi Salname-si"* (Bosphorus Yearbook) published by the Şirket-i Hayriye ferryboat company says that Beylerbeyi and İstavroz were two distinct neighbouring areas, İstavroz referring to the area between Beylerbeyi Kasır and the quay, and Beylerbeyi to the remainder.

Leaving aside the issue of the name's origin, the most significant aspect of Beylerbeyi was its function as an imperial estate throughout the Ottoman period. In the 17th century Ahmed I (1603-1617) and Murad IV (1623-1640) were both frequent visitors here, staying in lodges built for their use. Ahmed III (1703-1730) and his successor Mahmud I (1730-1754) were even more fond of Beylerbeyi, and restored and enlarged the existing buildings on the estate. A description of Beylerbeyi during the reign of Ahmed III reveals that there was a complex of structures here including an ornamental fountain flowing into a pool, tiled and domed pavilions, a prayer room, a Turkish bath with glass panes, a pavilion with a şadırvan (fountain for ablutions) overlooking the pool, a domed building with a view of the sea for the Valide Sultan (sultan's mother), a small two-floor building for the sultan's favourite wife, accommodation for the women servants and housekeeper, a pavilion for a female reader of the Koran, an Imperial Kasır (small summer palace or lodge) under the pistachio trees, a hunting gate, and a pavilion for the janissary commander on the waterfront.

In 1734, the boathouse was enlarged and the gardens laid out anew, and in 1735 a new köşk was built. The following year Mahmud I apparently spent several weeks here. Between 1740 and 1748 large sums were spent on building and alterations at the palace complex in Beylerbeyi. In 1760, the palace furniture was repaired.

Despite the effort and expense which went into perfecting this summer palace, Beylerbeyi's popularity waned in the second half of the 18th century to the point where Mustafa III (1757-1774) had the palace demolished and sold off the land. The curious reason given for this sale was that a house standing adjacent to the palace prevented it being enlarged. According to the bostancıbaşı's records for 1802, the only remaining imperial structures here were İstavroz Mosque and the nearby quay.

The late 18th and early 19th centuries mark a turning point in the history of the Ottoman Empire. Uprisings toppled the reformist and music-loving Selim III from the throne, to be succeeded by Mahmud II. The subsequent murder of Selim III so grieved his young nephew Mahmud II, that he could no longer bear the associations of Topkapı Palace. Wishing to break with the past and escape the memory of his uncle's death, he sought a site for a new palace. Beylerbeyi was finally selected, and the land which had previously been sold was repurchased, and construction of a new palace began. The contemporary historian Lütfî records that the owners of the land sold it to the sultan of their own accord. In 1828 documents record shipments of timber from İğneada to Beylerbeyi, and in 1829 various building stones arrived. Construction of the timber palace commenced in 1829 and was completed in 1832, according to Pertev Paşa's *"Tarih-i Berây-ı Sahil Saray-ı Beylerbeyi"* (History of the Waterfront Palace of Beylerbeyi). Evidence points to the fact that Beylerbeyi did not serve merely as a country residence for the sultan and his retinue, but was designed to take on the functions of government traditionally centred at Topkapı Palace.

In his memoirs Fieldmarshal Helmuth von Moltke, who was invited to İstanbul by Mahmud II as his military advisor, recalls that the state apartments (mabeyn) of the palace were divided from the palace proper by a high wall, that the palace covered a large area, and that it was painted light yellow. The following excerpt from Moltke's memoirs describes the gardens of the palace:

"By a gilded gate I entered a typical Turkish garden, with flowerbeds surrounded by boxwood hedges, and pathways sprinkled with seashells. Goldfish swam in the pools with fountains, around which were pyramids of cypresses and orange trees. Behind arose terraces, upon which were more

The Mermer Köşk, one of the buildings of Old Beylerbeyi Palace, and the bronze statue of a horse, thought to be a likeness of Sultan Abdülaziz's favourite horse Ferhan.

such places, beautiful greenhouses and pavilions; but the whole was surrounded by high walls...On the windows in the wall on the Bosphorus side were not only large grilles, but lattices of tightly woven cane. On the harem side these lattices were double-layered, and even on the third storey of the palace they covered the windows right to the top."

Elsewhere Moltke says that there was such a profusion of windows that the façade itself was virtually invisible, from which we can conclude that the palace was in keeping with traditional Ottoman palace architecture, although on a smaller scale. The historian Atâ gives us this account, which explains why the palace was of small dimensions:

"The sultans spend three or at most four months at this summer residence in privacy and seclusion with only as many palace servants as necessary. While Beşiktaş is big enough to accommodate the entire court, Beylerbeyi has been built on a smaller scale than this, and is insufficient to allow all the illustrious court to resort there."

Moltke was not the only one to speak of this palace built for Mahmud II. The famous French writer and Turcophil, Lamartine, records how he was passing by the palace in a caique and exchanged salutes with Mahmud II who was sitting by the shore at the time:

"I passed slowly by this palace, beneath whose gold and marble so many revelries, so many terrors were concealed. The sultan was seated on a couch in one of the waterfront pavilions. His young favourite Ahmet Paşa was standing beside him. Since our European dress had attracted his attention, the sultan pointed us out to Ahmet Paşa. I bowed in Turkish style to the sultan, and he returned it courteously. From the open windows of the palace shone the rich interior decoration of this magnificant and graceful building."

Abdülmecid, who succeeded Mahmud II, spent the first few days of his reign at Beşiktaş Palace before resorting to Beylerbeyi Palace, where he accepted the congratulations on his accession, indicating the important role played by Beylerbeyi Palace. In 1851, while Abdülmecid was still on the throne, a fire broke out here, and the sultan moved to Çırağan Palace for a brief while. Meanwhile the damage was repaired and in 1854 we find two banquets being held here, showing that Beylerbeyi Palace had by no means diminished in importance.

The only structures remaining from Old Beylerbeyi Palace are the Mermer Köşk-Marble Köşk and Beylerbeyi Tüneli-Beylerbeyi Tunnel. Although the Sarı Köşk-Yellow Köşk on the highest level of the terrace gardens has also been claimed to date from this period, research has proved that it was built at the same time as the new palace.

The Mermer Köşk is also known as the Serdab Köşk (serdab meaning a cool underground room for use in hot weather). This small three-roomed pavilion is set behind the large pool on one of the terraces. The design is typical of traditional vernacular architecture, and consists of a large marble sofa (a central room), flanked by two other rooms. The most distinctive feature of the köşk is the eliptical pool in the centre of the sofa. The water channels carved out of the marble flooring on either side of the pool link up to two fountains facing each other in the walls. The articulation and aesthetic devices created by the use of water as an architectural element in the interior is a tradition of longstanding. The railing which was installed around this terrace during the reign of Abdülaziz was removed during recent restoration. Clearly the köşk was built to provide a cool retreat in the heat of summer. Miss Julia Pardoe who visited İstanbul in 1836 described her impressions of this köşk and the small lake in front of it in her book *"Beauties of the Bosphorus"*:

"The finest portion of the grounds contains a noble sheet of water, called the Lake of the Swans, whose entire surface is frequently thickly covered with these graceful birds, of which the Sultan is so fond, that he sometimes passes hours in contemplating them as they glide over the still water... Boats, gaily gilded and painted, are moored under the shadows of the magnolias, willows, and other beautiful trees which form the framework of the lake; and about fifty yards from the bank stands a pretty, fanciful edifice, called the Air Bath - an elegant retreat from the oppressive heats of summer; whose roof, and walls, and floor, are alike formed of marble, wrought in marine devices; and whose fountains, trickling down the walls, pour their waters over a succession of ocean-shells, marine divinities, sea-weeds, and coral reefs; and keep up a constant current of cool air, and murmur of sweet sound, perfectly charming. Inferior apartments branch off on either side from this beautiful saloon, and altogether it is as pretty a toy as ever exhausted fancy in its invention."

The terrace gardens are one of the most distinctive features of Beylerbeyi Palace, rising in a series from the shore. Not only were terraces a traditional characteristic of Turkish gardens, but in this case the necessity of having the coast road pass through the grounds of the palace made terracing the logical solution. Whether Said Efendi, then supervisor of public works, played any role in devising this solution cannot be ascertained. In any event, a tunnel was constructed through which the road could pass, and the terrace gardens commenced above the tunnel. In this way the gardens on either side of the road were not divided. Carriages bringing visitors to the palace are thought to have used the gates inside the tunnel, within which is a wall fountain. The inscription on this fountain, which until recently was concealed by soil, has now been uncovered to reveal a poem inscribed by

The lake referred to by Miss Pardoe as the Lake of Swans and the Mermer Köşk. In her memoirs she notes that the sultan sometimes passed hours in contemplating the swans as they glided over the water.

the calligrapher Yesarizade Mustafa İzzet. One of the lines is a mnemonic formula (in which numerical values are attached to the letters of the Arabic alphabet) giving the date as 1245 AH (1829 AD) and the name of Sultan Mahmud who built the fountain:

"*Cedvel-i âb-ı hayatı kıldı Mahmud Han revan*"

(This channel of the water of life was made to flow by Mahmud Han).

On the fountain at the mouth of the tunnel is a poem by Hilmi.

Clearly Beylerbeyi Palace and the terrace gardens exerted a memorable impression on visitors to Istanbul, as we see from Miss Pardoe's account of her visit:

"*A marble gate, terminating the terrace in the direction of the city, admits the visitor into a garden bright with flowers, and redolent of perfume; where fountains for ever fling their delicate jets of water against the sky, with a soft and soothing music well suited to the spot; and where birds of gorgeous plumage wander at will, as rainbow-tinted as the blossoms amid which they sport. A line of gilt lattices veils the seaward boundary of this delicious retreat; and, passing beside these, an inlaid door of stately proportions gives admittance to the Hall of Entrance.*

"*The first glance of the interior is not imposing. The double staircase, sweeping crescentwise through the centre of the en-*

trance, contracts its extent so much as to give it the appearance of being insignificant in its proportions; an effect which is, moreover, considerably heightened by the elaborated ornaments of the carved and gilded balustrades and pillars. But such is far from being the case in reality; as, from this outer apartment, with its flooring of inlaid woods, arabesqued ceiling, and numerous casements, open no less than eight spacious saloons, appropriated to the Imperial Household. Above this suite are situated the State Apartments; gorgeous with

opposite page *The fountains in the pool and against the interior walls of the Mermer Köşk illustrate the way in which water was used as a decorative element in Ottoman architecture.*
below *Beylerbeyi Tüneli; an interesting architectural feature remaining from the Old Beylerbeyi Palace, which was built by Mahmud II.*

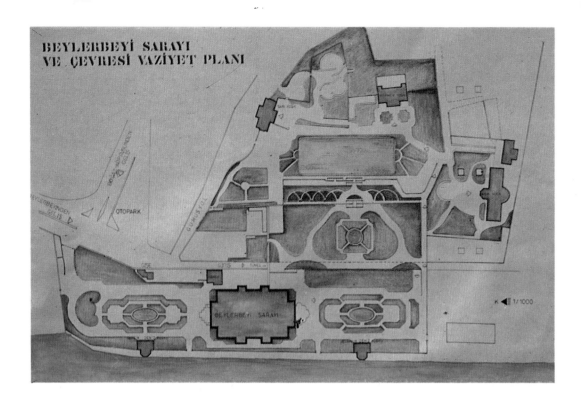

Site plan of Beylerbeyi Palace. The independent units of the palace are dispersed freely over the site, without any attempt to impose symmetry.

gilding, and richly furnished with every luxury peculiar alike to the East and to the West... We have now only to notice the extensive and princely gardens, which rise, terrace above terrace, to the very summit of the mountain which overhangs the palace. Each terrace is under the charge of a foreign gardener, and arranged according to the fashion of his own land... A gilded kiosque glitters amid the group of cypresses and plane-trees by which the last height is crowned; and the artist has ably portrayed the magic beauty of the scene which is mapped out beneath him as he stands beside the boundary-wall of the palace garden. The undulating shores, belted with houses, and sheltered by richly-wooded hills - the castle-crowned rocks - the gleaming sails of the passing vessels upon the channel - and, far away, the 'storm-tossed Euxine', lashing its billows as if in scorn against the fortress-barriers that bristle its shores - all combine to form a picture well calculated to arrest the eye of the painter and the admiration of the tourist."

Sentimental as this account by a western observer who was enamoured of İstanbul's oriental aspects might be, the information about Old Beylerbeyi Palace and its gardens are invaluable to researchers.

The Old Palace is Demolished
Frequent fires were the greatest ravager of the Ottoman architectural heritage, particularly in İstanbul where the

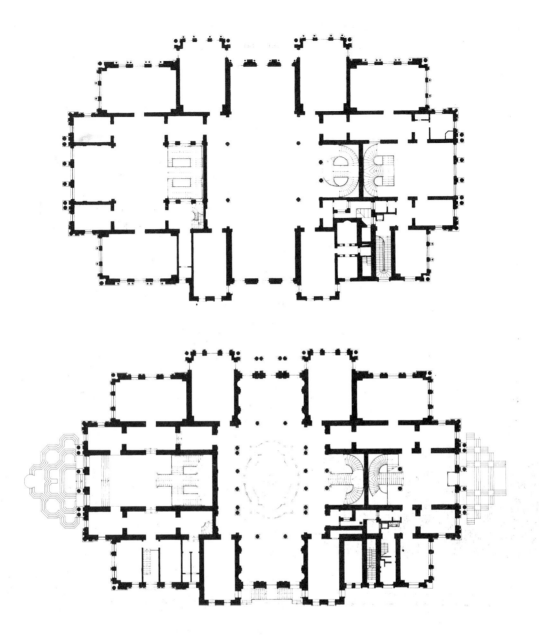

use of timber was prevalent. Countless palaces, köşks, kasırs and houses have been burnt to ashes, leaving only their names and stories behind. Fires affected the lives of sultans as well as the ordinary people, and it was this fear which prompted Sultan Abdülaziz to have the timber palace of Beylerbeyi demolished in 1851, and a new palace built of stone on the site. Presumably the Mermer Köşk was allowed to remain standing since it was made of fireproof marble.

above *Plan of the upper floor.*
below *Plan of the lower floor.*
The main palace building, consisting of 24 rooms, 6 reception rooms and connecting areas, retained the traditional layout of Turkish vernacular architecture despite the westernised appearance of the façade.

A NEW PALACE FOR A NEW ERA

*T*he historian Lütfî Efendi wrote the following account of the construction of the new palace:

"Beylerbeyi Waterfront Palace, which had been under construction for some while, was then completed and furnished to perfection, becoming a summer residence that year. On the fifteenth day of the month of Zilkade, the Friday selamlik ceremony was held as an act of piety at Beylerbeyi Mosque, after which a splendid procession proceeded to the Waterfront Palace where the imperial presence transformed this palace into an imperial

seat."

Construction of the new palace, which was designed by Sarkis Balyan, was the subject of a news item in the newspaper *Takvim-i Vekayi* on 28 Zilhicce 1281 (1864-1865). The article concluded with by the following lines by the poet Lütfi in commemoration of the event:

> *"This new waterfront palace of unequalled beauty was*
> *brought to life*
> *The sublime grace of his majesty Abdülaziz Han*
> *Lütfi presents his congratulations with his bejewelled history*
> *May God on high grant prosperity to this imperial palace "*

Evidently Abdülaziz attached great importance to this

While not covering such an extensive area as İstanbul's earlier palace complexes, the new palace built by Sultan Abdülaziz was still dispersed over a fairly wide area, and is a distinctive feature of the Bosphorus scenery.

palace and its decoration. According to documents in Dolmabahçe Palace archive, the sultan requested that the interior be decorated with heavily gilded fresco work, which was commissioned to the imperial painter Mason Bey.

The documents specify that the ceilings of the sultan's private apartments be decorated in heavier gold leaf than on the ceilings of the Büyük Camlı Kasır at the Imperial Palace of Beşiktaş, with naturalistic pictures of animals and birds. The ceilings of the rooms of secondary importance were to be decorated and gilded in the fashion of the upper storey ceilings of the Imperial Malta Kasır, but more elaborately. Finally the decoration of the lower storey

rooms were to be similar to the corresponding rooms of the Imperial Palace of Sadabad. The palace was to be illuminated by gas lamps, for which purpose a gasworks, of which no trace remains today, was built on Nakkaş Caddesi.

Yet despite all the pains taken to decorate the palace, it apparently remained unused until the French Empress Eugénie stayed here during her state visit in 1869, according to Dorina L. Neave who lived in İstanbul between 1881 and 1907.

The new palace was more compact than İstanbul's earlier palaces, which consisted of very extensive complexes of buildings, but nevertheless Beylerbeyi had numerous smaller structures spread over its grounds: Deniz Köşkleri-the Sea Köşks, Sarı Köşk-the Yellow Köşk, Paşa Dairesi-the Paşa Apartments, Ahır Köşk-the Stables, Muzika Dairesi-the Music Apartments, Geyiklik-the Deer House, Aslanhane-the Lion House, Güvercinlik-the Dove Cote, and Büyük Kuşluk-the Aviary, as well as the Mermer Köşk and the Lake.

left *Harem Yalı Kapısı-The Harem Waterfront Gate and Yalı Köşk-Sea Köşk. Designed as a summer palace, transport to Beylerbeyi Palace was generally by sea, so the Yalı or Deniz Kapısı-Waterfront Gates were the magnificent main entrances to the palace.*
above *The Ottoman coat of arms carved in stone surmounts Selamlık Yalı Kapısı-the Selamlık Waterfront Gate.*

THE DESIGN OF BEYLERBEYI PALACE

*O*ne of the most distinctive characteristics of Ottoman palace architecture was that having determined the general layout of the complex, the palace evolved with the addition of new buildings as need and taste dictated.

This characteristic continued until the 19th century, when changing social attitudes and western influences began to affect palace design. As a result, most of the palaces built in the 19th century were designed as a whole, as can be seen in Dolmabahçe and Çirağan palaces, as well as Beylerbeyi Palace. All the units of this palace were designed and built according to their individual functions within a predetermined layout.

As a summer palace, Beylerbeyi did not have to be as large as Dolmabahçe Palace, which was permanently inhabited, and the number of ancillary buildings was reduced to a minimum.

The independent units of the palace are arranged asymmetrically on the site. The main building is close to the shore, and the others dispersed around the terrace gardens and the lower grounds. The Sarı Köşk and the Mermer Köşk are next to the lake, while Ahır Köşk are to the south below them. Several of the buildings have disappeared entirely, such as Paşa Dairesi, Muzıka Dai-

above *19th century Ottoman architecture stressed the monumentality of palace buildings. The Mabeyn entrance to Beylerbeyi Palace is an imposing illustration of this.*

opposite page *Sultan Abdülaziz is known to have been fascinated by lions, as testified by the numerous statues of lions in the garden of the new palace which he built.*

24

resi, Geyiklik, Tavukluk-the Chicken House, and Aslan-hane. Large sections of the grounds have been allocated to various institutions, and the construction of the pier of the Bosphorus suspension bridge stands on land that

was formerly part of the palace grounds. Despite so many adverse changes, however, the palace proper and what remains of its grounds give us an idea - imperfect though it might be - of its original state, and even today Beylerbeyi is one of the distinctive features of the scenery along the Bosphorus shores. In Sedad Hakkı Eldem's *"Boğaziçi Anıları"* (Memories of the Bosphorus) he writes: *"This palace with its parkland behind which stretches along the shore, linked to the waterfront by high walls and graceful köşks has a distinct*

opposite page *The façades of Beylerbeyi Palace are striking examples of the eclectic architecture and decoration of the period.*
above *Detail of the façade decoration.*
below *Decoration on the roof parapet.*

The Corinthian columns and window pediments on the façade reflect the 19th century fascination with earlier architectural styles.

place within the natural setting. Although its proportions render it a focal point of its surroundings, the marble mass does not seem out of proportion within the surrounding greenery. The ancillary buildings of various dimensions are freely dispersed architectural elements which complement the right and left wings of the palace, contributing to the overall composition. The köşks of diverse sizes sprinkled on the hillside which climbs behind toward Çamlıca provide the resting points which the eye requires.

"The architecture of Beylerbeyi Palace, which was built several years before Çırağan Palace, is mellower and the Graeco-Roman elements more numerous. However, the engaged columns at the corners distance the overall composition from the classical order. Fantasies of greater dimensions can be observed in the waterfront köşks, which are set in the garden wall in a way quite unlike that at Çırağan. The garden walls which are a rhythmic extension of the right and left façades of the palace, provide a good visual support to the building."

The 19th century Beylerbeyi Palace illustrates the dis-

above *Twin columns with Corinthian capitals, arched windows, decorated bracket and details of the cornice.*
left *Detail of the façade decoration.*

opposite page *Twin columns on the seaward façade.*
above *Neo-classical column capitals.*

tinct western influence on Ottoman architecture over this period. The industrial revolution was gathering momentum, and the establishment of factories in and around major cities was attracting rural labour, leading to the erosion of traditions, customs and aesthetic values. The sense of alienation arising from urban life prompted a new nostalgia for the past. Contemporary urban architecture reflects this in the widespread use of elements taken from architectural styles of the past, such as Greek, Roman, Renaissance and baroque.

This trend in 19th century western architecture exerted a considerable effect on the Ottoman Empire, which looked to the west as a model. The many European architects who worked in Türkiye during the 19th century also played a part in this influence, which is clearly seen in the palaces of Dolmabahçe, Çırağan and Beylerbeyi.

Beylerbeyi, whose external appearance reflects contemporary western architectural style, consists of a basement and two main storeys, containing 24 small rooms

and six salons. In contrast to the exterior, the interior plan complies with traditional Turkish vernacular architecture, just as the western motifs of the exterior decoration gives way to traditional Turkish motifs in the interior. Mustafa Cezar expresses this phenomenon in the following words:

previous page *The entrance hall of the Mabeyn displays a synthesis of eastern and western styles.*
above *The cornice bearing the motif of a knight's helmet above the side doors of the entrance hall of the Mabeyn.*
right *Ceiling decoration in the entrance hall of the Mabeyn.*
opposite page *The staircase in the entrance hall of the Mabeyn.*

right *A vase in the waiting room adjoining the entrance hall.*
opposite page above *Detail of the decoration on the chairs. Not only the wall and ceiling decoration, but the furnishings, too, reflect the taste of the period.*
opposite page below *The miniature balcony and the doors lend a fascinating spatial articulation to the landing above the entrance hall of the Mabeyn.*

"The columns in Beylerbeyi do not have composite capitals created by the use of elements of the Doric, Ionic and Corinthian orders as at Dolmabahçe, but have been inspired by the mukarnas (stalactite work) of Islamic architecture to create a unique style. The decoration on the frieze, which is in harmony with these capitals, the ceiling and wall decoration, and the geometric coffering on the ceiling inspired by the designs of traditional Turkish woodcarving, testify to the attainment of a distinct level of originality in this building."

The palace is divided into two main sections, the Harem or private apartments and the Mabeyn or state apartments, each of which have separate entrances. While the architect preferred angular lines for the steps leading in-

above left *View of the reception room on the upper floor of the Selamlık.*
opposite page below *Another view of the same room. The mirrors set on opposite walls create interesting spatial illusions.*
above *A vase in the same room illustrates the use of porcelain as an architectural element.*
right *Detail of decoration on a cabinet in the same room.*

opposite page above left *Detail of the decoration in the corner of the ceiling of the reception room on the upper floor of the Selamlık.*
above *Decorated frieze around the ceiling. In contrast to the conspicuous western influence in the exterior decoration, Turkish and oriental motifs prevail in the interior.*
opposite page below *The reception room on the upper floor of the Selamlık.*
right *Clocks are among the objects used as decorative devices.*

to the Harem, those of the Mabeyn are curved. This contrast continues in the interior, the decoration of the Mabeyn being more ostentatious than that of the Harem. The personal interest which Abdülaziz took in the decoration, specifying what form it was to take in which rooms, is seen in the documents mentioned above.

The same close attention was paid to the selection of furnishings, which were purchased from Europe through the mediation of Briston and Parson. Furnishings were not only imported for the main building, but for the Sarı Köşk, Mermer Köşk and Deniz Köşks. Evidently the sultan took a rather different approach to this palace and its furnishing than to Dolmabahçe.

The entrance hall of the Mabeyn is covered with rush matting, as are the entire floors of the palace, and over this lies a large and valuable Hereke carpet. Off this splendid entrance hall with its large Sevres vase and Bohemian crystal chandelier, opens the Aide-de-Camp

The wall panelling which was a feature of Renaissance palaces has been used at Beylerbeyi Palace, but here the motifs are predominantly oriental.
left *View of the panelled room, number 18, in the Selamlık.*
opposite page above *A porcelain bowl with a finial in the shape of a bird on the lid, in the same room.*
opposite page below *Another view of the same room.*

Room, and an antechamber used as a waiting room for guests on the seaward side. The rooms opening off the hall to the landward side are plainer, and thought to be for the use of palace officials.

On the lower storey the Mabeyn and Harem are divided by a large reception room containing a marble ornamental pool, a traditional feature of oriental architecture.

Meanwhile, the fountains in the form of dolphins intro-
duce a western baroque effect, creating a synthesis typical of 19th century Ottoman architecture. One of the
rooms opening off the Pool Salon on the Mabeyn side is
that known as the Kaptan Paşa Room (Room of the Admiral of the Fleet). The naval theme of the room is
echoed in the rope motif on the furniture and the decora-

above *Detail of the wall decoration.*
below left *Detail of the table.*
below right *Detail of the chairs.*

tion on the walls and ceilings, reflecting the keen interest in the sea and naval affairs felt by Sultan Abdülaziz, who furthered the development of the Ottoman navy during his reign.

Access to the upper floor of the Mabeyn is via two staircases, one leading from the entrance hall and the other from the Pool Salon. Both are in an extremely ornate baroque style. The Ceremonial Room and Audience Room on the upper floor clearly illustrate the care and effort which went into the design of this palace. The latter is the last room before entering the Harem section of the palace.

Comparison with the design of Dolmabahçe Palace

opposite page *The dining room of the Harem. Sultan Abdülhamid's name is inscribed in Kufic script on the backrest of the chair.*
above *Detail of the marquetry on the window frames.*
below *The dining room of the Selamlık.*

previous pages *The furnishings of the Pool Salon, which divides the Mabeyn from the Harem, is largely decorated with traditional Turkish motifs.*
above *Detail of the statue of Abdülaziz.*
right *The statue of Abdülaziz, who had Beylerbeyi Palace built, in the Pool Salon.*
opposite page above *The marble dolphins of the baroque fountain in the Pool Salon.*
opposite page below *Another view of the Pool Salon.*

shows that the lay-out of Beylerbeyi Palace derives from the same funda-mental concept. The Zülvecheyn Salon at Dolmabahçe corre-sponds to the Selamlık (Ceremo-nial) Room at Bey-lerbeyi, while the room off the Zül-vecheyn at Dol-mabahçe where the sultan conducted his official affairs, corresponds to the Audience Room at Beylerbeyi. Thus the sultan was able to conduct affairs of state during his residence at Beylerbeyi, even though the palace was on a much smaller scale.

The concept of the "Principal Room" (Baş Oda) distinguished by fabric-lined walls appears in all 19th

opposite page *The Pool Salon.*
above *The seaward recess in the Pool Salon.*
right *Floral geometric motifs on the silk upholstery of the chairs and sofas.*

opposite page above *The staircase leading from the Pool Salon to the Blue Salon is a masterpiece in terms of structural design and decoration.*
opposite page below *View of the Pool Salon from the staircase.*
above *Another view of the staircase.*
left *Detail of the marquetry on the banisters.*

century Ottoman palaces, as it does at Beyler-beyi, where the rooms on the seaward side of the upper floor are possibly the most fascinating examples of this type. Instead of fabric, they are panelled in the style of Renaissance period palaces. This is natural in view of the fact

left *The staircase linking the Pool Salon to the Blue Salon.*
above *The capital of one of the columns in the Pool Salon underpinning the staircase landing.*
below *The Blue Salon, the most magnificent room at Beylerbeyi Palace.*

opposite page above *Capital of one of the columns in the Blue Salon. The classical motifs of the columns on the façades are replaced in this room by motifs inspired by Islamic art.*
left *The riot of decoration linking the walls, ceiling, architrave and columns in the Blue Salon.*
below *The Blue Salon.*

that Beylerbeyi Palace was designed in the eclectic style which characterises architecture of the 19th century.

Another interesting feature of the upper floor of the Mabeyn is the small Prayer Room, whose walls and ceiling are adorned with religious inscriptions.

The large and richly decorated entrance hall of the Harem corresponds to that of the Mabeyn. Again rooms open

opposite page above *Detail of a chair and the marquetry on the wall in one of the rooms leading off the Blue Salon.*
opposite page below *Detail of a bracket on the wall of the same room.*
above *Painting of a ship on the ceiling in the same room.*
left *Door of the same room leading into the Blue Salon.*

Sultan Abdülaziz's interest in naval matters is conspicuous in this room. Known as the Kaptan Paşa (Lord High Admiral) Room, both the furnishings and decoration reflect a naval theme, down to the rope motif on the suite of furniture.

opposite page above *Picture of a ship on the ceiling of the Kaptan Paşa Room.*
opposite page below *Ceiling decoration in the same room.*
left above *Detail of the curtains and sofa.*
left below *Rope motifs around the mirror and table.*

off this hall to the landward and seaward sides, and a double staircase leads up to the first floor. The seclusion of the Harem is as strictly abided by at Beylerbeyi Palace as in all the Ottoman palaces.

Although contemporary documents do not allow us to determine which room in the Harem belonged to whom, it is conjectured that the room on the seaward side of the upper floor corridor must have been that of the valide sultan, the sultan's mother. When the Empress Eugénie visited İstanbul during Abdülaziz's reign, she is known to have stayed in room number 24 in the harem, and to have used the adjoining bathroom. Otherwise little is known about the allocation of the rooms, either during the reign of Abdülaziz or during the six years which the deposed

opposite page *A bedroom in the Harem.*
left above *Inscriptions on the ceiling of Sultan Abdülhamid's bedroom.*
left centre *Abdülhamid's study.*
below *Abdülhamid's monogram on the centre table in his study.*

Sultan Abdülhamid spent here prior to his death in 1918.

All the rooms and large salons of Beylerbeyi have been designed according to the functions and hierarchy of the palace and in an integral style, from the light fittings down to the smallest details.

It is notable that no provisions whatsoever seem to

opposite page above left *Detail of a chair in the Harem dining room. Inlaid with malachite and mother-of-pearl in walnut, and upholstered in morocco leather. The name Abdülhamid is inscribed in Kufic script on the backrest of this chair.*

opposite page above right *The Harem dining room. Abdülhamid II's initials are engraved on the pier-mirrors. The console tables are in the French Armoire à deux corps style, dating from the Late Renaissance period.*

opposite page below *Detail of the decoration on the pier-table in the Harem dining room.*

above left *Detail of the pier-table.*

above left *Sultan Abdülhamid's coat-of-arms on the glass doors of the cabinets.*

below right *Detail of the decoration on the pier-table.*

have been made for heating the palace. Possibly this is because the palace was intended purely for use during summer. The ornate wall decoration makes up for the lack of the large fireplaces which are such a distinctive feature of the magnificent rooms of Dolmabahçe Palace.

How Sultan Abdülhamid II heated the palace when he lived here under house arrest during the latter part of his life is a subject worth further investigation. Nowhere in the palace, including the rooms Abdülhamid and his family occupied, is there a flue to which a stove chimney might have been connected, and we can only conclude that they used braziers.

The Deniz Köşks on the palace quay, known respectively as the Selamlık Köşk (that on the Mabeyn side) and the Harem Köşk, are each fronted by a double colonnade

arranged in two rows of four columns. Roofed by a segmental dome, the pavilions consist of a single main room and a service room. While the decoration is similar to that of the palace, it is far lighter, as appropriate for a structure intended for reposing by the sea. In these structures the architect, Sarkis Balyan, has made his first trial of a design which was to take its full-fledged form in Çırağan Palace.

The Terrace Gardens are one of the
principal features of Beylerbeyi
Palace, and a typical example of late
Ottoman landscape gardening.
opposite page above left *View of the Terrace
Gardens.*
opposite page below left *Part of the steps
leading up to the Terrace Gardens*
above *The lake on one of the upper
terraces of the gardens.*
left *A lily in the lake.*

Ottoman Palace Architecture and the Sarı Köşk

As mentioned already, the traditional Ottoman palace was an organic structure which evolved over time with the addition of new buildings. This characteristic began to disappear in the 19th century, when the principal units were designed as an integral whole. Nonetheless, additions and alterations were frequently made in accordance with the wishes of the reigning sultan, as in the case of the Hareket Köşks and Saat Kulesi-Clock Tower built at Dolmabahçe Palace during the reign of Abdülhamid II (1876-1909), and the chimney of the central heating system and Kuşluk Köşkleri-the Aviary Köşks constructed by the architect Vedat Bey (Tek) in the back gardens of the same palace during the reign of Mehmed Reşad (1909-1918).

However, these additions are the exceptions to the rule. Generally speaking all the palaces built in the 19th century obey the concept of numerous separate units within a conceptual whole. In this respect, Beylerbeyi follows suit. The Sarı Köşk on the terrace gardens, the Ahır Köşk and similar buildings are typical examples of traditional palace composition.

The Sarı Köşk, named either after the colour of the

The Sarı Köşk is contemporaneous with the new palace, and complements it in terms of both its architecture and decoration.
opposite page above *Façade of the Sarı Köşk.*
opposite page below *Interior of the Sarı Köşk.*
left *Paintings of ships on the ceiling of the Sarı Köşk.*
below left *A vase in the Sarı Köşk.*

stone or of the paintwork, has been sited at a point which commands a view of not only the Bosphorus, but Çamlıca Hill and the Marmara Sea. In terms of both its architecture and decoration, it is complementary to the main building, and was clearly built contemporaneously. The köşk consists of a basement and two main floors. On

the ceilings are seascapes depicting ships carrying the Ottoman flag. The köşk was evidently intended to fulfill a
recreational function, and this is confirmed by the list of
furnishings which were to be imported from Europe for
the köşk. From this document we learn that the room to
the right was to be furnished with mirrors, console tables,
torchieres, sedir (fitted divan), chairs and armchairs,
couches, chandeliers and table, and the room to the left
with similar furnishings but no sedir.

The position of the Sarı Köşk facing the Harem section
of the palace on the fourth terrace suggests that it was
built for the private use of the sultan himself. Similarly it
is likely that the arched gateway opposite the Harem
courtyard gate was used by the inhabitants of the Harem
(the sultan's female relatives, close male relatives, and
children) on their way to the Sarı Köşk.

Ahır Köşk

The building which stands by itself a little beyond the
Mermer Köşk to the south of the terrace gardens is the

The importance attached to horses and the equestrian arts by the Ottomans was reflected at its most magnificent in the palace stables. The Ahır Köşk at Beylerbeyi Palace are one of the few palace stables to have survived.

opposite page left *The bronze statue of a horse in front of the Ahır Köşk is thought to be a likeness of Ferhan, Abdülaziz's favourite horse.*

above centre and right *Views of the interior of the Ahır Köşk.*

left *A lamp decorated with horse heads in the Ahır Köşk.*

Ahır Köşk, an interesting illustration of 19th century Ottoman equestrian culture.

Now regrettably overshadowed by the Bosphorus suspension bridge, this building on the lowest terrace of the garden displays some fascinating architectural features. The protruding section of the façade is an entrance hall with a broad glass-paned door and windows. The ceiling of this section is decorated with pictures of horses and other animals. From here a few steps lead down to the stable room, in the centre of which is a small marble pool. There are twenty stalls to the right and left, each fitted with a hay rack. The mounting block which used to stand in front of the Ahır Köşk was broken up and disposed of when the Naval College took over a large part of the palace grounds.

The Ahır Köşk of the Çinili Köşk-Tiled Köşk built by Sultan Mehmed II (1451-1481) in İstanbul and those of the earlier palaces in Bursa and Edirne have not survived. The Ahır Köşk of Dolmabahçe Palace, which were still standing until relatively recent times, were demolished to make way for İnönü Stadium in the 1960s, and nothing but their photographs remain. The Ahır Köşk of Topkapı Palace and Yıldız Palace, and this small stable building at Beylerbeyi are the only remaining royal stables. This is a great pity in view of the importance attached to horses and the equestrian arts in Ottoman history and culture.

below *The cortège which met Sultan Abdülaziz upon his arrival in Vienna on 27 July 1867.*
opposite page above *Sultan Abdülaziz's visit to the Gallery Ambras in Vienna.*
opposite page below *Sultan Abdülaziz at Gare de Lyon in Paris*

PEOPLE AND EVENTS AT
BEYLERBEYI PALACE

*A*lthough Beylerbeyi Palace was only inhabited for brief periods, usually during the summer months, it harbours memories of people who played a role in significant events during the last decades of the Ottoman Empire.

No doubt much remains to be discovered, but of the events which are well documented the visit of the Empress Eugénie of France in 1869 during the reign of Abdülaziz

(1861-1876) is one of the most interesting.

Sultan Abdülaziz Pays a State Visit to Europe

The Ottoman sultan was invited to the opening of the International Paris Exposition in 1867, and a brief digression into the political and social implications of this state visit is called for here.

The decision of Abdülaziz to pay this visit at a time when the Ottoman Empire was beset by serious problems, including rebellions in Crete and Herzgovina, was supported by the government. It was hoped not only that the visit might lead to treaties with the European powers which would solve some of the country's political difficulties, but also that it would be beneficial for the sultan to see for himself the innovations and progress achieved in Europe. The visit had wide ranging consequences, which are dealt with at length in histories of the period.

This was the first time that an Ottoman sultan had ever visited a foreign country, and as well as being an opportunity for Abdülaziz to see western European art and culture at first hand, it led to a series of events witnessed by Beylerbeyi Palace.

The sultan set out on 21 June 1867 and arrived in Paris on 30 June, where he was welcomed by Emperor Napoleon III. Upon his arrival at the Tuilleries, Abdülaziz made the acquaintance of the Empress Eugénie for the first time, and this encounter probably gave rise to the idea of the empress paying a return visit to İstanbul.

Empress Eugénie Visits İstanbul

The Empress Eugénie was the first foreign guest to stay at Beylerbeyi Palace. Her visit was made on behalf of Napoleon III, and she arrived on the steamship *Aigle* on 13 October 1869. When the *Aigle* anchored off Beylerbeyi Palace, a flotilla of Ottoman naval ships greeted the empress with a

above *The celebrations to welcom the arrival in İstanbul of the Empress Eugénie.*
opposite page below *Sultan Abdülaziz's visit to the Elysée Palace.*

salute. Abdülaziz sailed out to the ship in an imperial barge with 12 banks of oars, and boarded the ship to welcome her and accompany her back to the quay of Beylerbeyi Palace.

Abdülaziz was eager to ensure Eugénie's comfort by providing everything which he had seen at the palaces and banquets of Europe. However, the most serious obstacle was finding staff versed in European customs and manners. Cooks and confectioners were hired from France, and the sultan's maitre d'hotel, Marko, visited Paris to oversee the preparations. Tableware was hired for the guests, and forty European-style uniforms were ordered from the tailor Lori for the footmen. Tulle and a fringe for the edging of the bedspread were purchased for the bedroom being prepared for the empress, and 21 pairs of slippers and other items were also purchased for her use. Alterations were even made to the bathroom adjoining her bedroom. In short, vast expense and effort went into the preparations for this distinguished guest, at a time when French-Ottoman relations were still on a very amicable footing.

It appears that this effort was not wasted, however, and Eugénie left İstanbul with fond memories of the visit. When she returned to İstanbul 41 years later at the age

opposite page and above The Empress Eugénie of France with Sultan Abdülaziz at a ceremony in the Blue Room of Beylerbeyi Palace where she stayed during her visit to İstanbul. Engraving after a sketch by M. Chelebovski.

The bedroom and bathroom prepared
for the Empress Eugénie of France at
Beylerbeyi Palace. Atatürk later
stayed in this room during his visit
to the palace.

of 85, she asked to revisit Beylerbeyi Palace. Sultan Mehmed Reşad (1909-1918) gave the necessary permission, and instructions were issued by the Imperial Treasury specifying the refreshments which should be provided to the royal visitor at the palace. Although the emotions of the empress can only be guessed at, Halit Ziya Uşaklıgil who accompanied her remarked in his memoirs that she appeared moved.

Famous Guests

The Empress Eugénie was not the only famous guest to stay at Beylerbeyi Palace. She was followed by the Emperor Joseph of Austro-Hungary in 1869, Şah Nasıreddin of İran in 1873, and Prince Nicholas of Montenegro in 1874. Grand Duke Nicholas, sent by Czar Alexander II following the Russian victory in the Ottoman-Russian war of 1874, also stayed here, and Crown Prince Oscar of Sweden visited the palace in 1891.

Sultan Mehmed Reşad gave a banquet for the members of parliament and the Senate in the garden of Beylerbeyi Palace.

The last guest at the palace during the Ottoman period was Sultan Abdülhamid II.

Abdülhamid II's Last Home

The story of Beylerbeyi Palace during the Ottoman period ends with the six-year stay of Sultan Abdülhamid following three years in exile at the Alatini Köşk in Salonika. After being deposed in 1909, Abdülhamid was sent into exile in Salonika, but in autumn 1912 when the fall of Salonika to the Balkan forces was imminent, Abdülhamid was brought to İstanbul on the *Lorelei* and settled in Beylerbeyi Palace. His arrival is recorded by his daughter Ayşe Osmanoğlu in her memoirs:

"When my father disembarked on the quay and walked towards the door of the Mabeyn, the guard barred his way and shouted 'Forbidden'. 'I had not thought,' said my father, and turning towards the Valide Gate of the Harem, he entered the palace. As soon as he entered he remarked to Nuri Ağa who was behind him, 'Nuri, how damp this place is. It will be the death of me.' 'My lord, why do you speak so?' Nuri Ağa replied. At which my father said, 'It was here that my mother died.' Then he walked straight to the room which he was to use as his bedroom thereafter. 'My mother used to sleep here. I will make this my bedroom.' And he had his possessions brought into the room."

Abdülhamid lived here in the Harem until his death on 10 February 1918. He had a bathroom installed nextdoor to his bedroom, as we learn from Ayşe Osmanoğlu:

"With a pleased smile, my father said, 'My bathroom is ready. Now I will be comfortable. In truth Rasim Bey has expended great efforts. Enver Paşa's father Ahmet Paşa used to

understand such things. He came and we discussed it togeth-
er. I asked for Karlo Usta, who built my bathrooms at the pal-
ace according to my own plans. They found him and brought
him here. He did a very good job. Now I am content."

Yet it was this bathroom which eventually brought about Abdülhamid's death. During a serious illnes he insisted on bathing despite remonstrances to the contrary, and while in the bath he collapsed and had to be helped back to his room, where he died three days later.

BEYLERBEYİ PALACE DURING
THE REPUBLICAN PERIOD

Atatürk and Beylerbeyi
With the establishment of the Republic in 1923, the palaces, köşks and kasırs which had once belonged to the Ottoman imperial family had to be put to new uses. Ankara had become the capital of Türkiye and the seat of government, although the caliphate was preserved until 1924. The last heir to the Ottoman throne, Abdülmecid Efendi, was appointed Caliph and settled in Dolmabahçe Palace. However, when he became inclined to resume some of the privileges of the sultanate, parliament passed an act abolishing the caliphate on 3 March 1924. Abdülmecid Efendi was informed of this decision by Governor of İstanbul Haydar Bey on 4 March 1924. The property of this last representative of the Ottoman dynasty reverted to the state, including Beylerbeyi Palace, which came under the auspices of the Turkish Grand National Assembly.

Following the War of Independence, Atatürk paid his first visit to İstanbul on 1 July 1927 and gave a speech in the Muayede Salon (Throne Room) of Dolmabahçe Palace, at which he declared that the palaces were now the property of the Turkish nation, and that he himself was a guest there.

For a few years Beylerbeyi Palace was used to accommodate distinguished guests to Türkiye, among them Şah Rıza Pehlevi of İran in 1934, for whom a banquet was held in the Pool Salon. In 1936 the Balkan Games Festival was held at Beylerbeyi Palace, during which Atatürk stayed in Room 24, where the Empress Eugénie had stayed nearly 70 years earlier. Atatürk was the last guest ever to stay here.

*B*EYLERBEYI PALACE
AS A MUSEUM

*F*ollowing the National Palaces Symposium held in 1984, preparations to open the palaces to the public gathered momentum. Following restoration of the Mermer Köşk and Stables, these buildings and the terraced gardens were opened to visitors on 5 July 1985. Soon afterwards the Sarı Köşk followed suit, the garden in front of it being used for children's art courses, and the lower floor for slide shows and similar activities. The upper floor was equipped as a venue for conferences and meetings. Once the main palace and the tunnel were opened to the public, Beylerbeyi Palace became the first major museum on the Asian shore of the Bosphorus. Programmes of cultural activities were organised at Beylerbeyi, as at the other palaces, köşks and kasırs under the auspices of the Department of National Palaces.

Opening to the public this beautiful and unique palace, in its lovely setting on the shore of the Bosphorus, was a long overdue event. Against the backdrop of its terrace gardens and lake, whose theme of water as a decorative element is repeated in the palace interior, Beylerbeyi Palace is a museum-palace which illustrates many facets of Turkish history and culture.

BIBLIOGRAPHY

AHMET LÜTFİ EFENDİ, *Lütfi Tarihi*, Vol. IV, X, (Editör: MÜNİR AKTEPE) AKDTYK Pub., Ankara 1988

Prime Ministerial Archive, Cevdet Saray Collection No. 608, 1040, 2102, 2253, 3354, 4245, 4703, 5189, 5362, 5544, 6361.

Prime Ministerial Archive, Maliye İradeleri No. 14310

CEZAR, MUSTAFA, "Sanatta Batıya Açılışta Saray Yapıları Ve Kültürünün Yeri", *Milli Saraylar Sempozyumu/Bildiriler*, İstanbul 1985, pp. 39-61.

CEZAR, MUSTAFA, "Batıya Açılış Döneminde Mimaride Bünye Değişikliği", *Milli Saraylar Dergisi* 1987, No. 1, pp. 12-21.

CEZAR, MUSTAFA, "Süslemeler Yönünden Dolmabahçe Ve Beylerbeyi Saraylarına Bir Bakış", *Milli Saraylar Dergisi*, 1992, No. 2, pp. 4-26.

ELDEM, SEDAD HAKKI, *Boğaziçi Anıları*, İstanbul 1979.

ERDOĞAN, MUZAFFER, "Osmanlı Devrinde Boğaziçi Bahçeleri", *Vakıflar Dergisi*, 1958, No. 4, pp. 149-182.

EVLİYA ÇELEBİ, *Evliya Çelebi Seyahatnamesi*, Vol. 15 (Transcribed by: ZUHURİ DANIŞMAN), Danışman Pub., İstanbul 1969-1971.

GÜLSÜN, HAKAN, *Dolmabahçe Sarayı Ve Mimar Vedat Bey*, İstanbul University, Dept. of Art History, unpublished thesis, İstanbul 1990.

İNCİCİYAN, P. G., *18. Asırda İstanbul*, (tr by: H. ANDREASYAN), İstanbul 1956.

KARAHÜSEYİN, GÜLLER, "Beylerbeyi Sarayı Ve Ünlü Konukları", *Milli Saraylar Dergisi*, 1992, No. 2, pp. 122-138.

KONYALI, İ. HAKKI, *Üsküdar Tarihi*, Vol. I, İstanbul 1976; Vol. II, İstanbul 1977.

KÖMÜRCÜYAN, E. Ç., *İstanbul Tarihi, 17. Yüzyılda İstanbul*, (tr. by: H. ANDREASYAN), İstanbul 1952.

MOLTKE H. Von, *Türkiye'deki Durum ve Olaylar Üzerine Mektuplar (1835-1839)*, (tr. by: H. ÖRS), Ankara 1960.

OSMANOĞLU, A., *Babam Abdülhamit*, İstanbul 1960.

RADO, ŞEVKET, "Bostancıbaşı Defteri Hakkında", *Hayat Tarih Mecmuası*, 1972, No. 6.

SÖZEN, METİN, *Devletin Evi Saray*, Sandoz Kültür Pub., İstanbul 1990.